Written by

Sylva Nnaekpe

Copyright © 2020 Sylva Nnaekpe.

All rights reserved. No part of this book may be reproduced by any means, medium, graphic, electronic or mechanical, including photocoping, recording, taping or by any information storage retrival system without the written permission of the author except in the case of brief quotations embodied in critical articles and reviews.

Books may be ordered through bookstores or by contacting Silsnorra llc at:
silsnorra@gmail.com

Due to the dynamic nature of the internet, any web address or links contained in this book may have changed since publication and may no longer be valid. The views expressed in this work are solely those of the author and do not necessarily reflect the views of the publisher, and the publisher hereby disclaims any responsibility for them.

ISBN: 978-1-951792-71-8 (Soft Cover)
ISBN: 978-1-951792-70-1 (Hard Cover)
ISBN 978-1-951792-72-5 (Electronic book)

Printing information available on the last page.

Silsnorra llc Review Date: 01/19/2020

I see colors everywhere I go.

1

I see blue sky.

I see a gray walkway.

I see a yellow school bus.

9

I see purple eggplants.

I see brown hazelnuts.

I see pink roses.

21

I see white sand.

I see goldfish.

I see the yellow sun.

I see colors everywhere I go.

29

Now, look around you.

What colors do you see?

COLOR WHALE

THE END

Follow @ ivrydbook
to see more.